# James, the Brother of Jesus
*by James Byers*

## HILLIARD
PRESS

## James, the Brother of Jesus

Published by Hilliard Press
a division of The Hilliard Institute
Franklin, Tennessee
Oxford, England

# Table of Contents

# Introductory Remarks

In 2002 an ossuary was discovered in Israel allegedly containing the remains of James the brother of Jesus. *Biblical Archaeology Review* editor Herschel Shanks led a defense of its authenticity.

This discovery led to a renewed interest in this rather obscure person and his contributions to early Christianity.

James is mentioned in Matthew 13:53–58 as one of the brothers of Jesus.

The theory accepted by many Christians is that this James is the half-brother of Jesus as Joseph and Mary had other children after the Savior's birth.

Another theory from several sources espoused by Origen, Eusebius, and Ambrose as well as Epiphanius is that James is the son of Joseph by an earlier marriage (with Mary being the second wife of Joseph). According to this view, Mary being the exception, the whole family at Nazareth was not of blood relation to Jesus. It is a conception in the interest of the dogma of the perpetual virginity of Mary. The advanced age and decrepitude of Joseph start with that premise. This is the official teaching of the Roman Catholic Church.

A lesser-known theory states that the Greek word for brother, *Adelphos*, can be translated as *kinsman* or *cousin*. This was first propounded by Jerome and several Roman Catholic writers and was accepted by some leaders of the Reformation including Luther.

James and his brothers remained skeptical that Jesus was the Messiah (John 7:5).

What changed James from skeptic to a full believer? Paul records that Jesus appeared to James as well as the apostles after His resurrection (I Corinthians 15:3–8).

After the Ascension, we find James, the apostles, Mary, and others praying continually (Acts 1:12–14).

To examine James, one must begin with the early years of Jesus Christ. In my research, I used various translations including *The New Testament Contemporary English Version.*

# The Early Years

The earthly siblings of Jesus are not mentioned in the early chapters of the gospel writers. The nativity story focuses on the mother of Jesus in Luke's gospel and the earthly father of Jesus in Matthew's gospel. Luke documents Mary's encounter with Gabriel, an angel of God who tells her she is going to conceive and give birth to Jesus (Luke 1:26–33). In this encounter Mary insists that she is not married and by inference has not had sexual relations (1:34). In fact she immediately visits her relative Elizabeth for comfort and most assuredly advice after Gabriel's message (1:39–40). Gabriel told Mary that Elizabeth is with child even though she is past the age of normal child bearing (1:36).

Later as Luke records the journey of Joseph with Mary to Bethlehem for the purpose of a census, there is no mention of any children with them on the journey or provisions made for care for children when the couple leaves Nazareth. Luke plainly indicates that Jesus is the only child in the birth story (2:1–6).

After the birth of Jesus and as the days approach for Mary's purification rites, Jesus is portrayed as the only child in the family. A sacrifice is made as befitted a working class family (2:22–24). During this time a prophet by the name of Simeon blesses Jesus and praises God. After the prayer Simeon states that he can die in peace, as the Spirit of God told Simeon he would not die until he had seen Jesus. The praise of Simeon is beautiful in tone and mentions that Jesus will save not only His people but foreign nations. Simeon mentions the mighty power of God that will be a light to all nations. Simeon also has a special prophecy for Mary, which predicts her future suffering similar to a stabbing by a dagger. At the same time a prophet by the name of Anna is in the temple. Anna comes to the couple and praises God. She talks about the child Jesus who will set free Jerusalem (2:25–38).

Thus in these early days of Jesus' infancy, no mention is made of siblings being present or being cared for by others. Luke records no more events in the young years of Jesus with the exception of His trip to Jerusalem. At age twelve, Jesus journeys with His parents to Jerusalem for the Passover feast. No mention is made by Luke of other siblings on this Passover journey. In fact the story indicates that Jesus is beginning to see His purpose as His distraught parents find Him sitting with religious teachers. The story ends with Jesus going back to Nazareth with His parents. Luke makes clear that Jesus remains subject to His parents' authority (2:41–51). Mary is shown as a thinker about all that happens (2:51). Luke closes the chapter with the conclusion that "Jesus became wise, and He grew strong, God was pleased with Him and so were people" (2:52). Again in this story, no mention is made of siblings.

When one turns to Matthew's gospel, no mention of Jesus' siblings is noted in the nativity section. This gospel begins with the genealogy of Jesus and traces His lineage back to Abraham. Matthew conveniently divides the genealogy into three sections: fourteen ancestors for each section. As Matthew observes, there are "fourteen generations from Abraham to David. There were also fourteen from David to the exile in Babylonia and fourteen more to the birth of the Messiah" (1:17).

Matthew concentrates on Joseph, the earthly father of Jesus. The narrative avoids any suggestion that Joseph was previously married with children. Rather, Matthew's message revolves around the impending marriage of Joseph to the maiden by the name of Mary. The ancestry of Joseph is emphasized with the statement that he is a descendant of King David (1:1–16).

Joseph is also mired in a great dilemma when he learns that his Mary is pregnant. Some Biblical translations indicate that Joseph has an annulment of marriage in mind. Matthew adds that Joseph is a just man who does not want "to embarrass Mary in front of everyone" (1:19). In Matthew's account the Holy Spirit explains to Joseph in a dream the miracle of Jesus' conception. The explanation includes the admonition to name the male child Jesus, "because He will save His people from their sins" (1:20–21).

After the birth of Jesus, wise men from the east visit: "On coming to the house, they saw the child with his mother Mary, and they bowed down and worshiped Him" (2:11). Notice Jesus is called a child and not a baby—and still no mention is made by Matthew of other children in the family of Joseph and Mary.

Matthew then relates the warning of the angel to Joseph. This warning comes in a dream and concerns the danger from the King of Judea, Herod. Matthew writes, "That night, Joseph got up and took **his wife and the child** to Egypt where he stayed until Herod died. So the Lord's promise came true, just as the prophet had said, 'I called my son out of Egypt'" (2:14–15). The bold is added in the above scripture to note the singular mention of offspring.

When Joseph returns to Galilee, his family lives in the town of Nazareth. Matthew refers to another prophecy, "So the Lord's promise came true, just as the prophet had said, 'He will be called a Nazarene'" (2:23). In this family return to Nazareth, Matthew does not mention siblings, only "the child and his mother" (2:21).

We have no early mention of brothers or sisters, leaving a mystery and several conjectures as to when the siblings of Jesus were born. Were they living before the birth of Jesus and reunited at some point? Or were they born after Jesus, making them the children of Joseph and Mary?

Matthew very plainly states that Joseph and Mary had marital relations after the birth of Jesus (Matthew 1:25). This would be normal in any culture. However, in Christian beliefs today, two main suppositions have endured. The first conjecture is that these siblings were children of Joseph by a previous marriage and older than Jesus. This logically would place Joseph much older than Mary and explain that Joseph may have died before the ministry of Jesus. Joseph is not mentioned in the company of Jesus after the Passover journey in Jesus' twelfth year.

After reading the infancy accounts in both gospels, the reader naturally wants to know more. But to ask questions about the siblings of Jesus often leads to futility. The reader is not given full biographies in most of the biblical stories. In the Old Testament, Joseph (son of Jacob) occupies a large amount of space in Genesis, but the reader does not encounter this Joseph's story until he is seventeen years of age. Little is known of his years in prison until he is elevated to Pharaoh's court. His biography is measured by his service to his God and his resistance to evil.

Other patriarchs are known for their obedience and faith. Speculations have been made about Abraham's beginnings, but his real story appears later when he is tested in his faith in Yahweh. The patriarchal stories are encased in theological teachings.

When one questions the story of the siblings of Jesus, great vacuums are present. If one takes the view that the siblings are the children of Joseph and Mary, then the reader avoids the problem of a celibate marriage. As has been mentioned, the New Testament (in Matthew 1:25) supports a normal marriage relationship between Joseph and Mary. The view of the perpetual virginity of Mary demands a celibate marriage.

Most scholars today believe the conjecture that Joseph and Mary had children. The children would then be younger than Jesus. They would not accompany Jesus to the Passover when Jesus was twelve years old. One solution to this situation would be that they stayed with other relatives while the trip was made. Jesus' family, at least from His mother's side, was complex. Many scholars believe that Mary, the mother of Jesus, and Salome, the wife of Zebedee, were sisters. With this view, James and John, the future apostles, were cousins of Jesus and were also related to the family of John the Baptist (John 19:25).[1] Thus, as was the custom of those days, children often stayed with relatives when needed. This could have been the case at the time of the Passover trip.

During His youthful years, Jesus and His siblings must have experienced normal family relations. From all indications, Joseph and Mary's household was a typical Jewish home.

Joseph, whose occupation or trade was carpenter, served as the spiritual leader of the home. Luke summarizes the growth of Jesus in four different areas—wisdom, stature, favor with God, and favor with man (2:52)—and this must have included His relationship with brothers and sisters.

Jewish youth always learned a craft or trade as part of their maturation. Woodworking or carpentry was the craft of choice for Joseph and his male children. We can securely assume that Jesus and His brothers learned the trade very early in their lives. Wooden pulpits were used even in Ezra's time when he read the law from one (Nehemiah 8:4).

In Matthew 13:55–56, the writer records Jesus visiting His hometown of Nazareth: "Isn't he the son of the carpenter? Isn't Mary his mother, and aren't James, Joseph, Simon, and Judas his brothers? Don't his sisters still live in our town?" Joseph is known for his craftsmanship. It would be fair to assume that his sons at least learned carpentry. Usually families were known as purveyors of a trade as there were no giant malls or stores in small towns. If one wanted carpentry work done, he or she would go to the appropriate trade family.

The early years of Jesus and His male siblings would have been spent in an apprentice-like atmosphere learning this craft. The female siblings would have learned crafts such as sewing, embroidery, and cooking. The male siblings such as Jesus and James would have attended synagogue school. Jesus had already shown great aptitude for matters of the Jewish Law when He is mentioned as "sitting in the temple, listening to the teachers and asking them questions. Everyone who heard him was surprised at how much he knew and at the answers he gave" (Luke 2:46–47).

Beyond the apprentice and synagogue years, one cannot account for the life of Jesus until His ministry. His last appearance before His ministry is the trip to Jerusalem at age twelve. Thus the so-called "missing years" continue to remain a matter of speculation to the reader of scripture. At some point in those years Joseph disappears from the gospel stories. The conjecture has long been that he died before the years of Jesus' ministry. The brothers, including Jesus, care for or are close to Mary. She continues to live in Nazareth and is well-known by the town.

# The Ministry Years

James, the brother of the Lord, or "ho adelphos tou kuriou," is mentioned in the gospel writings on several occasions. One of the first is a visit by Jesus to the synagogue in Nazareth, and another is the visit of Jesus to Capernaum when James attempts to persuade Jesus to travel to Judea. Another occasion occurs when Mary, the mother of Jesus, appears with Jesus in Cana in John's gospel. John carefully details a wedding feast at this village and notes that Jesus and His disciples are there: "This was Jesus' first miracle, and He did it in the village of Cana in Galilee. Then Jesus showed His glory, and His disciples put their faith in Him. After this, He went with His mother, His brothers, and His disciples to the town of Capernaum, where they stayed for a few days" (John 2:11–12).

The miracle consists of turning water into wine, and the identification of the disciples could logically include the chosen twelve. Verse twelve of this chapter indicates that, after this occasion, Jesus, His mother, brothers, and disciples went to Capernaum. Thus, His brothers may have been at the wedding feast, or they could have joined Him later as they traveled to Capernaum.

The question could be asked as to who are these brothers? When the term brethren is used in Matthew's gospel (Matthew 12:46–50), commentator Alfred Plummer identifies these brothers as the children of Joseph and Mary: "There is nothing in Scripture to forbid the natural view that these 'brothers' are the children of Joseph and Mary, born after the birth of Jesus." Concerning Jesus, Plummer adds, "His devotion to His mission involved separation from even His mother and His brethren. Of the latter we know that they did not believe in Him (Jn. VII.5), a fact which is conclusive against any of them having been among the Twelve Apostles." [2]

As previously mentioned, a passage of scripture that is often cited as occurring very early in Jesus' ministry is found in Luke the fourth chapter when Jesus delineates His mission and reads from the Isaiah scroll: "The Lord's Spirit has come to me, because He has chosen me to tell the good news to the poor. The Lord has sent me to announce freedom for prisoners, to give sight to the blind, to free everyone who suffers, and to say, 'This is the year the Lord has chosen'" (Luke 4:18–19). Those who are in attendance at the synagogue where the reading took place are amazed as they knew Jesus as the son of Joseph (4:20).

In the same setting, Matthew records a detailed skepticism from these same townspeople: "He taught in their meeting place, and the people were so amazed that they asked, 'Where does He get all the wisdom and the power to work these miracles? Isn't He the son of the carpenter? Isn't Mary His mother, and aren't James, Joseph, Simon and Judas his brothers? Don't his sisters still live here in our town? How can He do all this?' So the people were very unhappy because of what He was doing" (Matthew 13:53–57).

Mark uses similar words: "Jesus left and returned to His hometown with His disciples. The next Sabbath He taught in the Jewish meeting place. Many of the people who heard Him were amazed and asked, 'How can He do all this? Where did He get such wisdom and the power to work these miracles? Isn't He the carpenter, the son of Mary? Aren't Jesus, Joseph, Judas, and Simon his brothers?' The people were very unhappy because of what He was doing" (Mark 6:1–3).

These passages show the rejection of Jesus by the people of Nazareth and the presence of a mother and siblings who lived in Nazareth as well. As Plummer states concerning the miracle at Cana, there is little evidence that Jesus' siblings, including James, are believers in His Messiahship at this time. Jesus' mother expresses faith in His power to perform miracles such as the one at Cana (John 2:1–4). She also ponders or thinks deeply at the events of His early years. How much she believes in His Messiahship at this point is unclear. Jesus' brothers are not even disciples, as Plummer observes. Their faith in Jesus appears suspect.

However, Mary and the siblings continue to be very protective in regards to Jesus. John writes in detail about the family's attempt to persuade Jesus to leave Judea:

> Jesus decided to leave Judea and to start going through Galilee
> because the leaders of the people wanted to kill him. It was time
> for the Festival of the Shelters, and Jesus' brothers said to Him,
> "Why don't you go to Judea? Then your disciples can see what you
> are doing. No one does anything in secret, if they want others to
> know about them. So let the world know what you are doing!"
> Even Jesus' own brothers had not become His followers. Jesus
> answered, "My time hasn't yet come, but your time is always here.
> The people of the world cannot hate you. They hate me, because I
> tell them that they do evil things. Go on to the festival. My time
> hasn't yet come, and I am not going." Jesus said this and stayed on
> in Galilee. (John 7:1–9)

Mark recalls another occasion when the family of Jesus misunderstands Him and believes they can help: "Jesus went back home, and once again such a large crowd gathered that there was no chance even to eat. When Jesus' family heard what He was doing, they thought He was crazy and went to get Him under control" (Mark 3:20–21).

Matthew records another occasion when Jesus is speaking:

> While Jesus was still speaking to the crowds, his mother and
> brothers came and stood outside because they wanted to talk with
> him. Someone told Jesus, "Your mother and brothers are stand-
> ing outside and want to talk with you." Jesus answered, "Who is
> my mother and who are my brothers?" Then He pointed to His
> disciples and said, "These are my mother and my brothers! Anyone

who obeys my Father in heaven is my brother or sister or mother."
(Matthew 12:46–50)

All of these scriptures share the element of family concern. In Matthew the
concern is not as clear. Jesus seems to be harsh with His family. In reality He
expands His ministry beyond family ties to include even separation from His
mother and siblings.[3]

The Mark passage clearly reflects concern regarding the mental state of Jesus.
His family obviously thinks He has suffered physical and mental exhaustion
and wants Him rescued from the great crowds.

The passage in John is concerned with both safety and exposure to more important audiences. In John's account Jesus has limited exposure to audiences
in Judea. However, a danger is present in that region because His life would
be in peril. His brothers advise Jesus to go to Judea for the exposure to great-
er crowds. B. F. Westcott thinks that John is referring "not only to those disciples who would be gathered from all parts to Jerusalem, but especially those
who had been gained by earlier teaching in Judea and Jerusalem, and who
still remained there. From this notice it appears that miracles were wrought
chiefly among strangers to arrest attention and also that the Lord was accompanied only by a small group of followers in His Galilean circuits."[4]

John adds the mysterious comment that not even His brothers believe in
Him (*ouk episteuon*). This passage has always troubled readers since Jesus was
part of an extended family who were from the same town and who undoubt-
edly saw some of His works which they advised Him to display outside of
Galilee. F.L. Godet gives an even more detailed explanation stating that the
brothers "are perplexed with regard to the claims of Jesus; on the one hand,
they cannot deny the extraordinary facts of which they are every day the
witnesses; on the other they cannot decide to regard as the Messiah this man
whom they are accustomed to treat on terms of the most perfect familiari-
ty. They desire, therefore, to see Him withdraw from the equivocal situation
which he creates for Himself. And in which He places them all by keeping
Himself so persistently at a distance from Jerusalem. If He is truly the Messiah, why indeed should He fear to make His appearance before more com-

petent judges than the ignorant Galileans? His place is at Jerusalem. Even at this time, six months before the last Passover, Jesus' own brothers did not acknowledge Him as the Messiah."[5]

Other scholars have weighed in on James' loyalty to his brother. The author, John Painter, concludes that James and the other siblings were followers of Jesus by their presence with Him. Painter categorizes the disciples of Jesus as both ideal and less than ideal. James, at this time, was less than ideal.[6] The puzzling scene at the crucifixion includes the "beloved disciple" John and also Jesus' mother. His mother's sister and Mary Magdalene are there. The glaring absence of Peter and other disciples is troubling but cannot be labeled as complete unbelief. Painter describes the absent witnesses of the crucifixion as "having suffered a failure of nerve…and they have fallen short of the response of the ideal disciple."[7]

The conclusion reached from the gospel accounts is simply that James and his siblings as well as the majority of the disciples were frightened, dismayed, and uncertain. The rejection of Jesus by Peter haunted Peter for life. James and his siblings would later undergo a transformation. However, their collective weaknesses did not mean that they had completely abandoned discipleship. Both Painter and Jeffrey Butz, who authored *The Brother of Jesus and the Lost Teachings of Christianity*, agree that from the beginning the family of Jesus were followers of Jesus in various ways. Yet the fire of zeal had not been refined. The events following the crucifixion would have a profound effect on their lives. James, the Lord's brother, would undergo a complete change.

# The Resurrection

The resurrection of Jesus Christ is recorded in all of the gospels. Various individuals are mentioned as seeing the resurrected Lord. The individual accounts are in a certain sequence, but the exact order of Jesus' appearance cannot be determined. The first appearance is to various women who came to the tomb where Jesus was buried (Matthew 28, Mark 16, Luke 24, John 20). This type of post-death visit was normal as the Jewish custom was to anoint the body for several days.

John's gospel highlights Mary Magdalene. What is known about this Mary is first recorded in Luke 8. The commentator Leon Morris notes that Jesus attracted certain women because He chose to teach them: "The rabbis refused to teach women and generally assigned to them a very inferior place. But Jesus freely admitted them into fellowship, as on this occasion, and accepted their service. First to be mentioned is Mary, called Magdalene. The Christian imagination has made free with Mary Magdalene, mostly seeing her as a beautiful woman whom Jesus had saved from an immoral life. There is nothing whatever in the sources to indicate this. Luke says that seven demons had gone out from her, which shows that Jesus had rescued her from a very disturbing existence. But there is no reason for connecting the demons with immoral conduct: they are more usually associated with mental or physical disorder."[8]

Mary Magdalene becomes an ardent follower of Jesus along with several other women. Luke mentions Joanna, Susanna, and many others. These women help support Jesus' ministry and may have financed Him with considerable resources as Joanna's husband Chuza was one of Herod Antipas' officials (Luke 8:2–3). Mary Magdalene leaves her home in Magdala, which is near the Sea of Galilee. The place can easily be seen today from a tour boat while sailing on the Sea of Galilee. Her devotion is permanent, and she is found at the crucifixion site with other women: "Many women had come with Jesus from Galilee to be of help to Him, and they were there, looking on at a distance. Mary Magdalene, Mary the mother of James and Joseph, and the mother of James and John were some of these women" (Matthew 27: 55–56).

Among the personal appearances of the resurrected Jesus, only Luke tells the story of the two despondent disciples who are travelling to the village of Emmaus. Henry Wansborough in his commentary calls the story Luke's most memorable.[9] Luke describes the disciples as gloomy and sad. Jesus suddenly joins them on their foot journey to the village, explains to them the meaning of His own death and resurrection, and tells them the history of the scriptures, which includes the Mosaic Law and the writings of the prophets. As they stop with Jesus to share an evening meal, He reveals Himself to them as the Messiah. They are immediately overwhelmed. When He suddenly disappears from their company, the disciples reflect, "When He talked with us along the road and explained the scriptures to us, didn't it warm our hearts?" (Luke 24:32).

In I Corinthians 15:5–8, Paul mentions individually the resurrection appearances of Jesus to Peter and James as well as his own visionary experience as he journeyed to Damascus. John records Peter's experience in length with the admonition of Jesus to Peter: "When Jesus and His disciples had finished eating, He asked, 'Simon son of John, do you love me more than the others do?' Simon Peter answered, 'Yes Lord you know I do!' 'Then feed my lambs,' Jesus said" (John 21:15–19). This exchange goes on three times, the same number of times Peter had denied Jesus. Peter's experience with the resurrected Jesus is one of wonder and contrition.

The resurrected experience with Paul is extraordinary as Paul sees a great light and a voice from heaven. This voice explains to him to cease his persecution of Christians. Paul experiences days of anguish until he is ready to completely change his life (Acts 9:1–19).

In the particular experience of James, who is identified as the brother of Jesus, the details of the resurrected appearance of Jesus are not revealed. One can only conclude that his unbelief is changed to complete belief. James no longer considers Jesus as just his earthly brother. He now considers Him his Lord and Savior. This transformation of the resurrected Christ dramatically changes the lives of these witnesses. Paul, the great apostle, writes that Jesus appears to more than 500 in His resurrected body (I Corinthians 15:6–7). With James, as well as the others, lives are changed forever. James's life can be validated as extremely influential in the beginning years of the church. Luke records more about James as church leader in the Book of Acts.

# James, Leader of the Church

Luke, author of the Book of Acts, mentions the brother of Jesus in the first chapter: "The apostles often met together and prayed with a single purpose in mind. The women and Mary the mother of Jesus would meet with them, and so would his brother" (Acts 1:14). In the early days and weeks, it appears that the apostles led the small assembly in worship.

The last message Jesus gives His apostles occurs after they question Him about His future plans including the possibility of a king for Israel. "You don't need to know the time of those events that only the Father controls. But the Holy Spirit will come upon you and give you power. Then you will tell everyone about me in Jerusalem, in all Judea, in Samaria, and everywhere in the world" (Acts 1:8).

After Jesus' ascension, the apostles are told by angels to stop looking up in the sky—in other words get to work. Their first order of business is to replace Judas Iscariot who committed suicide after his betrayal of Jesus. Peter accepts a leadership role and describes in great detail the demise of Judas. He quotes from the book of Psalms: "Let someone else have his job" (Acts 1:20). Peter then describes the rules for selection. Number one is for the person to have been with them from the beginning and to have seen Jesus. Other requirements are the witnessing of His baptism and ascension.

Names are selected, and finally only two are considered: Joseph Barsabbas and Matthias, and the latter is drawn as the successor by the casting of lots. The number of apostles is twelve once again. It is evident that neither James nor any of the other brothers are considered for selection. We have validation that the brothers did not follow Jesus from the beginning and did not witness His baptism. Clearly at this early stage, James was not a leader in the church.

The Holy Spirit controls the apostles, and they speak to a great Passover crowd. The apostles are the leaders in the church, and Peter becomes their spokesman. Peter addresses the great Passover crowd with amazing results. Three thousand are baptized on the day of Pentecost (2:14–41). Truly from that day forward Peter becomes the leader of the church.

Luke clearly divides the Book of Acts into the Petrine mission and the Pauline mission. Both are preachers and leaders in the early church. In Luke's second chapter, he records that the followers of Jesus "often met together, and they shared everything they had. They would sell their property and possessions and give the money to whoever needed it. Day after day they met together in the temple. They broke bread together in different homes and shared their food happily and freely, while praising God. Everyone liked them, and each day the Lord added to their group others who were being saved" (Acts 2: 44–47).

Luke portrays the church of early days as meeting at times in the temple or, as F.F. Bruce identifies the place, in "Solomon's Colonnade." These disciples also met in private homes to have meals and fellowship. Bruce speculates that the breaking of bread could have included an ordinary meal, an Agape or love feast, and the Eucharist or Lord's Supper.[10] The beginnings of the church can be defined as very optimistic in that followers are not afraid to meet in large gatherings or in small groups, primarily private homes. R. B. Rackham observes that the followers of Jesus obey His teachings that "wealth was a loan from God of which we are stewards." These followers enjoy a period of tranquility in worship even after the death of Jesus. This tranquility lasts for only a short time, but Peter's sermon on the day of Pentecost lengthens the time of peace.

At this point the brothers of Jesus, including James, are not mentioned with the exception of Acts 1:14 where the writer states, "These all with one accord continued steadfastly in prayer, with the women, and Mary the mother of Jesus, and with his brethren." Rackham notes the lack of church "organization."[11] This group of disciples is not yet called Christians, yet they follow Jesus the Christ. They share worldly goods and care for one another. They meet with regularity at different places. They enjoy fellowship. Most importantly at this point in time, the followers of Jesus have a great orator: Peter. Peter and his companion John form a great missionary team. With boldness they preach the Gospel, which includes Jesus Christ crucified and resurrected. These spokesmen seem no different from the other followers except they have the gift of the Holy Spirit to proclaim their message as no others could. Peter and John even amaze the members of the Sanhedrin, the Jewish high court (Acts 4:13).

At this point in time, the followers of Jesus begin to be a threat to established religion. In spite of the danger, the early church continues to grow. Even quite wealthy people become disciples, sharing their wealth and selling many of their possessions to give support to the apostles. Clearly some of the apostles were forming an organization within the disciples of Jerusalem. A landowner by the name of Barnabas becomes a prime example of a wealthy man giving freely to finance the gospel mission. This man, who is known not only for his generosity but also his gift of exhortation, becomes one of the leaders of the young Jerusalem church.

Peter continues to assert the primary leadership in this early period of the church in Jerusalem. He disciplines Ananias and Sapphira, two members of the fellowship, for their fragrant lying (Acts 5). He and John and other apostles continue their ministry but at some time agree that delegation of sacred duties has to be practiced. Thus Luke records the appointment of "seven men who are respected and wise and filled with God's spirit," so that the apostles, as they say, "can spend our time praying and serving God by preaching" (Acts 6:3–4). "These men were brought to the apostles. Then the apostles prayed and placed their hands on the men to show that they had been chosen to do this work. God's message spread, and many more people in Jerusalem became followers. Even a large number of priests put their faith in the Lord" (Acts 6:6–7).

Noticeably absent from these assistants to the apostles are James, the brother of Jesus, and James's brothers. Luke continues the early history of the Jerusalem church with the story of Stephen, one of the seven chosen men. Stephen is the first to die for his faith after he preaches a very comprehensive oration to the Sanhedrin (Acts 7). Luke also documents the conversion of an important Ethiopian official taught by Philip, another one of the seven chosen men (Acts 8:26–40), and records the conversion of Saul (Acts 9), later known as Paul, who was introduced earlier as one of those who participated in the execution of Stephen (Acts 7:58).

The Book of Acts continues with the evangelization of Cornelius, who is a God-fearing man and a Roman army officer. Peter converts this Roman and his household members and explains his ministry to Gentiles to the Jerusalem church (Acts 10). Jerusalem continues to remain the home church of the disciples of Jesus. As far as can be seen, James and his brothers are members of this church.

The Jerusalem church becomes upset that Jesus is being preached to Gentiles. Luke observes in Acts 11:1–3 that the "apostles and the followers in Judea heard that the Gentiles had accepted God's message. So when Peter came to Jerusalem, some of the Jewish followers started arguing with him…'You stayed in the homes of Gentiles, and you even ate with them!'" By the end of Peter's story of the conversion of Cornelius, the followers stop arguing among themselves and start praising God. They say, "God has now let Gentiles turn to Him, and He has given life to them" (Acts 11:18).

One can assume that James also had concerns about the Gentiles that were alleviated by Peter's report. About this time a healthy alliance forms between the Jerusalem church and the newly established church in Antioch of Syria. The church in Antioch starts because many followers of Jesus are scattered to friendlier places after the persecution that begins with the martyrdom of Stephen.

Peter continues his missionary activities with the other apostles. Luke records the great trauma in the apostolic leadership when James, the brother of John, is executed by Herod Agrippa, the grandson of Herod the Great (Acts 12:2). During this period of great stress Peter is imprisoned by Herod, and his execution seems certain. The followers of Jesus intensely pray for Peter's safety. These followers meet in the house (*oikion*) of John Mark's mother, most likely a large home complete with servants. Peter is miraculously released from prison by an angel of God and walks to the house of John Mark (12:6–16). As Bruce observes, this house church is surprised "to believe that their own prayers had been answered so quickly" as they listen to "Rhoda's (a servant girl) insistence that it really was Peter–while all the time the poor man himself stands anxiously knocking for admission."[12]

Is James, the brother of Jesus, ever at this prayer vigil? The answer seems to be no, but he is certainly aware of the imprisonment. By this time James would have been a vital member of the Jerusalem church. Bruce comments that among the house churches of Jerusalem, James would be revered. "Although not one of the Twelve, and indeed not a believer until the Resurrection, he had apostolic qualifications as a witness of the risen Christ." His spiritual maturity is demonstrated later when he "acts more or less as chairman" of a conference in Jerusalem.[13]

The year of Peter's imprisonment is in the early 40s AD. After his release, Peter makes a significant statement to the disciples at John Mark's residence. "Peter motioned for them to keep quiet. Then he told how the Lord had led him out of jail. He also said, 'Tell James and the others what has happened'" (Acts 12:17). Peter then goes someplace else. From these words we can see the need for the house churches to remain underground—Peter did not want great excitement at his release and left the assembly quickly. Also, James is to be told of the events that had happened. This James is obviously the brother of Jesus because James, the son of Zebedee and brother of John, had recently been executed.

After Herod Agrippa's death, the persecutions of the Jerusalem church are more restrained, even eliminated, for a period of time. Luke introduces a new missionary team consisting of Barnabas, Saul (or Paul), and John Mark. Barnabas, who had already been to Antioch, helps bridge any gaps between the followers in Antioch and the church in Jerusalem. Barnabas also goes to find Paul, after he became a Christian, and brings him to Antioch. Antioch becomes the more active missionary church—the followers of Jesus are first called Christians there. Antioch seals its friendship with the believers in Jerusalem by sending financial aid during a terrible famine. Luke writes that the Christians in Antioch have "Barnabas and Saul take their gifts to the church leaders in Jerusalem" (Acts 11:30).

James must have approved of all this activity, and he remains as the one who would receive the gifts in Jerusalem. Then, at some point, James becomes a primary leader in the great church of Jerusalem. In his essay on "James and Jesus on Israel and Purity," Scott McKnight concludes, "a more careful examination of the data shows that James was indeed a significant figure, a (perhaps the) dominant leader of the Jerusalem Church and the spokesman for the earliest form of Jerusalem-based Christian Judaism. For instance, from Act 1:14 and 12:17 we can infer that the brothers of Jesus were both at the chronological basis of the Jerusalem churches as well as the core leaders of the movement."[14]

As James develops into a primary leader in Jerusalem, an evaluation of Jesus' family must be examined thoroughly. There is no indication that Jesus ever rejects His earthly family or that His earthly family is completely skeptical of His prophetic gifts. Why James and his brothers are not included in the original twelve can only be the subject of speculation. But this natural family of Jesus is never excluded from the family of believers in the Jerusalem church. As Painter points out very clearly, "Certainly Luke makes clear that the eschatological family, those who hear and do the word of God, is not restricted to the natural family, though the natural family are not excluded either"[15]

James is next mentioned as a counselor and arbiter in Jerusalem. While both Peter and Paul are involved in mission trips, James, from all indications, stays in Jerusalem. It would be extremely inappropriate to portray James as un-interested in any kind of evangelization. He had himself seen the mission of Jesus and concludes his thoughts on this phenomenon when he witnesses the resurrected Jesus. With the credential of being the earthly brother of Jesus, he naturally is the choice of other disciples to make ultimate decisions regarding the spiritual direction of the Jerusalem church. Many changes occur in the decades of the 40s and 50s AD. The church begins to look at this brother of Jesus for leadership. James is already replacing the role of Peter, who is often absent from Jerusalem. This transition proves to be amiable in nature. A first indication is Peter's request to inform James of his escape from Herod Agrippa's prison. The authority of James must have grown during these days, and, by the time that doctrinal differences and ethnic disputes arrived, James is the source of wisdom.

The significance of James's counsel is demonstrated in the great conference held at Jerusalem. The results of the decisions made at this conference will set the course of the Christian movement for future generations. As has been stated, by the time of Herod Agrippa's persecution, James is a leader to whom Peter confides. James is also a significant figure in regard to another great preacher. When Paul tells his conversion story to the Galatian disciples, he mentions that after his conversion in Damascus, he spent time in Arabia and Damascus. Paul reckons the time span as three years. He then recounts that he went to Jerusalem and spent fifteen days with Peter. This meeting becomes a significant memory for Paul who must have had doubts about his acceptance by the Jerusalem church. Then Paul mentions meeting James the brother of the Lord, and Paul describes James as an apostle (Galatians 1:19). This meeting shows that James has ascended to great prominence in the Jerusalem church. Paul speaks about when he returned to Jerusalem with Barnabas fourteen years later. He had come to Jerusalem with a clear message. At Jerusalem he met with the "pillars" of the church. A more modern translation explains:

> James, Peter, and John realized that God had given me the message about His undeserved kindness. And these men are supposed to be the backbone of the church. They even gave Barnabas and me a friendly handshake. This was to show that we would work with Gentiles and that they would work with Jews. They only asked us to remember the poor, and that was something I had always been eager to do. (Galatians 2:9–10)

James is listed before Peter and John in Paul's story. Earlier Paul is even more specific regarding his calling: "They [the leaders] realized that God had sent me with the good news for Gentiles, and that he had sent Peter with the same message for Jews. God, who had sent Peter on a mission to the Jews, was now using me to preach to the Gentiles" (Galatians 2:7–8).

In Galatians, one might question which *James* Paul is mentioning. William R. Farmer in his essay "James the Lord's Brother According to Paul" believes Paul is speaking about the Lord's brother in all three of the references to this name. Farmer states, "I wish to acknowledge that I think that Paul is referring to the same person in all three cases." By this time Farmer concludes that James is considered an apostle and that Paul's meeting with Peter and James in Jerusalem forms an advantageous alliance for the spread of the Gospel to both Jew and Gentile. Farmer observes that James is a leader who exerts influence in Antioch and in churches even more distant from Jerusalem including "the important Roman province of Galatia."[17]

More can be said about James and his emerging leadership in the early church because of his linguistic closeness to the words of his brother Jesus. As Farmer points out, James from childhood would have known the Aramaic idioms of his brother's language: "For this reason alone, as minor a consideration as it might appear to have been, James would have been highly respected by the other apostles, including those who had been Jesus' disciples, like Peter. On matters like this Peter would have deferred to James. Their apostolic partnership or concurrence on such a matter would have been important." The importance of James as a leader had a twofold basis of privilege: James was accepted as an apostle and as one of the Lord's brothers.[16] By the time of the conference in Jerusalem as recorded by Luke in Acts 15, James has established full credence by those assembled as arbiter and conciliator.

In his book *The Spreading Flame*, F.F. Bruce considers James's role at the conference a pivotal one. Bruce notices that Peter and the other apostles are increasingly absent from Jerusalem about ten years after the beginnings of the Jerusalem church. James's role as administrator increases as he remains in Jerusalem. Bruce acknowledges the success of the conference in that city mainly due to the wisdom of James. The success of the Antioch mission, which meant that there might soon be more Gentile Christians in the world than Jewish Christians, creates a serious problem. Bruce notes, "And it was in considerable part thanks to James' practical wisdom that a serious problem, which might have brought about an unbridgeable cleavage in primitive Christianity, was settled in a spirit of concord."[17]

The Jerusalem conference is without a doubt the largest gathering of church leaders in the twenty years after Pentecost. Luke states that "the apostles and church leaders met to discuss this problem about Gentiles" (Acts 15:5). Among those who met to discuss the problem were Paul and Barnabas from Antioch and the apostles and church leaders from Jerusalem. The apostles and leaders of Jerusalem must have included Peter, John, and James. Most scholars today date the conference at approximately 50 AD. Those attending had in some way been witnesses of the ministry of Jesus; thus the conference would never be surpassed in importance in its implications for the future of Christianity.

F.F. Bruce recognizes that problems had festered for several years. He cites Peter's refusal to participate in a fellowship meal with Gentiles, and Paul's subsequent criticism of Peter's hypocrisy. Bruce also mentions the early church experiences in regards to the mandatory observance of Jewish ceremonial law including male circumcision. Paul writes an acerbic letter to Galatian converts who are passively submitting to Jewish customs. Paul sees the Galatian heresy as "a radical contradiction of the good news which brought deliverance from sin."[18]

The Jerusalem conference thus would determine if Christianity can exist in an amicable manner between Jew and Gentile. The stakes are high because many of the new church congregations contain both Jewish and Gentile ethnic groups. After a persuasive testimony from Peter regarding his own experiences—the main experience being his visit to Cornelius the Roman Centurion and the conversion of Cornelius and his household—the other members of the Jerusalem church accept the inclusion of Gentiles (Acts 15:6–11). James also speaks and exerts his great wisdom and leadership (15:13–21). As Bruce comments, "James' ruling carried the day. It was decided that no other condition than faith in Christ should be imposed on Gentiles as necessary for salvation or for fellowship with their Jewish fellow-believers."[19]

The conference, under the supervision of James, adopts a compromise that allows for customs to be observed without Christianity being thwarted. Most of the imposed compromises are already observed at this time by all Christians, whether Gentile or Jewish: refraining from idolatry; adhering to strict morality including righteous behavior regarding sexual relationships; and not eating blood meat (Acts 15:28–29). This art of selective compromise works beautifully, and James's admonitions must have been received with great appreciation.

This compromise permits Paul and later on Peter to preach the Gospel as far away as Rome, perhaps even Spain. James, among others, stays in the area of Jerusalem, and these leaders adopt more Jewish attitudes. Whatever the case, James asserts his moral authority in a global way. His conduct at the conference shows a man willing to listen before giving advice. This conference also documents that James, above all other leaders, has the credibility as Jesus' brother to have words of authority. Even such stalwarts as Peter and Paul are satisfied with James's instructions. The early church, even though more Jewish in some areas and more Gentile in others, becomes one church. James, according to Bruce, "winds up the debate, and formulates the motion which he puts to the meeting." James progresses from an unbeliever to the foremost adviser of the Jerusalem church.[20]

After the historic conference in which James acts as counselor and decision maker, little is mentioned of him in the scriptures. In all likelihood James increases in importance not only in Jerusalem, but throughout the community of believers. With the inclusion of the Epistle of James into the New Testament canon, more evidence of his religious beliefs is revealed.

# The Epistle of James

The Epistle of James has been a source of controversy over many centuries. Martin Luther dismissed it as an inferior work because of theological difference on the topics of faith and works. In addition there have been several questions as to which James wrote the letter. Most scholars list four possible candidates; James, the son of Zebedee, and James, the brother of Jesus, are the two most serious contenders for the authorship.

James Zebedee is martyred early on in the history of the New Testament. His death occurs about 44 AD at the hands of Herod Agrippa. That leaves James, the brother of Jesus, as the strongest possibility for authorship.

J.W. Roberts in his commentary about the epistle strongly favors the brother of Jesus. Roberts emphasizes the close connection of family ties. "It may be safely concluded that James is an actual brother to Jesus in the flesh through the common mother, Mary."[21] Roberts concedes that, during the ministry of Jesus, James and other family members have their doubts as to the messiahship of Jesus but concludes the following:

> After the resurrection Christ appeared to James (I Cor. 15:7) and
> this seems to have changed all, for immediately it is noted that
> he was among the number who waited during the interval be-

fore Pentecost (Acts 1:13,14). James' attitude could be described as typical of Judaistic Christianity. First his Hebrew or Jewish background is taken as basic. But he is also seen in the dual role of championing the freedom of the Gentiles from the law (as Paul contended) while at the same time being zealous for the observance of traditional Judaism for Jewish Christians. This is probably to be interpreted as a measure of statesmanship aimed at winning his nation to the claims of the gospel.[22]

The Epistle of James continues to have doubters as to authorship. One objection is that the Greek is too good for a native of Israel. This doubt is based on the specious assumption that Jesus' family could not have known Greek because the family lacked educational opportunities. Obviously, Greek-speaking Jews are in the Jerusalem church as Luke describes in Acts 6. A conclusion would have to be made that not only James but Peter and John who also wrote letters in the New Testament did not know Greek. Without a doubt, translators were available when needed.

Another objection is that James makes few references to Jesus, only two in number, and never states the Lord is his brother. Yet these objections pale in significance when recognition is made of James's complete humility in regards to Jesus as Christ. Of course, by the time of the authorship of the letter, about 60 AD, everyone in the Christian community would recognize James as not only the brother of Jesus but the foremost leader of the Jerusalem church.

The letter or epistle itself is a model of practical Christianity. If one is a Christian, how must one conduct one's life? This question is thoroughly answered by James in various ways and in various situations. James has as his main concern a definition of the Christian life. His readers are a scattered group. They are of Jewish ethnicities and encounter everything from persecution to affluence. He devotes a large portion of his letter to admonishing his readers to a life of endurance to hardship. He encourages them to hold on to their faith and ask for wisdom.

James expresses a strong social benevolence, which he discussed previously in the Jerusalem conference. "But any who are rich should be glad when God makes them humble" (James 1:19).

If you have faith in our glorious Lord Jesus Christ, you won't treat
some people better than others. Suppose a rich person wearing
fancy clothes and a gold ring comes to one of your meetings. And
suppose a poor person dressed in worn-out clothes also comes. You
must not give the best seat to the one in fancy clothes and tell the
one who is poor to stand at the side or sit on the floor. That is the
same as saying that some people are better than others, and you
would be like a crooked judge. (James 2:1-4)

The Jewish social conscience is well described by James. God has a particular
concern for the downtrodden. James goes so far as to identify true religion as
ministering to the orphans and widows (1:27). These thoughts remind us of
the compassion that his brother Jesus had for the widows in His ministry. The
widow of Nain comes to mind.

Although Jesus did not condemn someone for being wealthy, He challenged
the rich to use their resources generously. As the commentator W.E. Oesterley writes, "According to Jewish teaching, there are certain works of obli-
gation; good works done over and above these are of free will, and by these
justification in the sight of God is attainable."[23] James also does not condemn
wealth, but he challenges the rich to use their wealth generously. He con-
demns senseless luxury and shows empathy for the poor. James addresses the
problems of both rich and poor.

James also concludes that the Christian must realize that "every good and
perfect gift comes down from the Father who created all the light in the
heavens. He is always the same and never makes dark shadows by changing.
He wanted us to be His own special people, and so He sent the true message
to give us new birth" (James 1:16-18). James reminds us of the words that
Jesus taught His disciples, and how He lived His life speaking and com-
muning with the less popular and less fortunate, when this writer reminds
us that we must love everyone and not treat some people better than others
(James 2:9).

Oesterley agrees with most scholars that the Epistle of James "is for the most
part a collection of independent sections,"[24] the most discussed sections being
in the second chapter. This section deals with the topic of faith and works—
or salvation by means of a working faith. James writes, "My friends, what

good is it to say you have faith, when you don't do anything to show that you really do have faith? Can that kind of faith save you?" (James 2:14). Though it might seem harmless, this verse has caused much controversy through the years. Many sermons have been preached extolling the virtues of faith while other sermons focus on rewarding the merits of works. J. W. Roberts targets the source of the problem: the relation of this section to the earlier parts of the letter should not be ignored. Jesus insists that true religion must show itself in proper response. It is not merely the hearer who is saved by the word, but the doer. Religious works or acts of service that do not find accompaniment in works of love and moral living are vain. Faith toward Christ must not be held with respect of persons, or the Christian becomes a sinner. James now shows that faith as the foundation attitude of the Gospel must find expression in works of obedience if it is to be a saving or justifying faith. If it does not, it is a dead faith—and the man who thinks that such faith will save is mistaken. There must be more than faith; works must help faith for it to achieve its purpose of justification.[25]

As regards salvation, James is obviously referring to works that are produced by faith. These works should naturally flow from one's belief in Jesus Christ. Paul concludes that faith, genuine faith, leads us "to do good things, and to live as He has always wanted us to live" (Ephesians 2:8-19).

James is teaching from a strong Jewish background. He provides many ingredients that compose an active faith. He illustrates the need to care for the poor, those without food or clothes. From Old Testament texts, he provides the examples of Abraham, who was willing to sacrifice his son Isaac if necessary; also Rahab, the prostitute who lived in Jericho, who "pleased God when she welcomed the spies and sent them home by another way" (James 2:25). James disregards what could be called intellectual faith by itself. He writes that even evil demons believe in God and fear Him, but they do not act in His will. James concludes that Abraham is the example of "faith and deeds" working together and that "anyone who doesn't breathe is dead, and faith that doesn't do anything is just as dead" (James 2:28).

In a summary of the epistle and the attitude toward working faith, we must remember that James's view of the hopeless and disenfranchised is paramount. Painter views James and his perspective: "The church down through the ages has needed to hear this challenge to take a stand on the side of the poor, weak, and powerless. The last word then is James the Just, James the Faithful, James the Righteous."[26]

The letter of James is not a letter that is neatly organized. Various topics relating to Christian conduct are discussed. Roberts thinks that all the various themes of the letter relate to James 1:19–27, much as a piece of music has various expositions of a central theme.[27] In this passage James centers Christian conduct on controlling anger and subduing evil, placing stress on obedience to the word of God. James encourages what he calls **true religion**. James talks about the controlling one's speech in the third chapter of his epistle. Arrogance and personal cruelty are strongly condemned in chapter four. The epistle in chapter five is full of warnings for the rich and exhortations to the humble. James 5:4 summarizes his thoughts: "You refused to pay the people who worked in your fields, and now their unpaid wages are shouting out against you. The Lord All-Powerful has surely heard the cries of the workers who harvested your crops." In James 5:6 he writes, "You have condemned and murdered innocent people who couldn't even fight back."

James teaches patience, kindness, and prayerful supplications. He admonishes his listeners, "If you are having trouble, you should pray. And if you are feeling good, you should sing praises. If you are sick, ask the church leaders to come and pray for you" (James 5:13–14), and "if you turn sinners from the wrong way, you will save them from death, and many of their sins will be forgiven" (James 5:20). In his summary of the thoughts in James's letter, Painter mentions that the teachings in James about God are "drawn from the riches of the Jewish tradition, rooted in an understanding of creation which finds itself confronted by evil and suffering. The Epistle of James has as its central concern a deep sympathy for the poor and persecuted. It advocates the rights of widows and orphans while offering a stern critique of the rich merchants and rich farmers."[28]

James shares the Jewish idea of the righteous person who will suffer and who will face temptation. The believer will face adversity just as the prophets, Job and Elijah to be specific, had. When looking at this type of language, we see James says many of the things that his brother Jesus had taught. Many subjects in James's letter were discussed by Jesus in His lifetime including The Law of Love; humility and exaltation; and relationship with brethren.

James's epistle is not in disagreement with Paul's gospel message. As previously stated, Luther dismissed the letter of James as inferior, an epistle of straw. However, Luther admired parts of the epistle. As readers today, the apparent theological differences between Paul and James can be resolved when looking at the working faith extolled by James. While primarily addressed to Jewish converts, James's epistle has now been more thoroughly understood as a truly "catholic" letter, a letter whose teachings affect all ethnic and social groups.

# Jude and James

Family relationships in the New Testament are extremely complex. James was a very common name as was Mary, John, and Judas or Jude. The names become a veritable genealogical Rubik cube in many cases. In the situation of the brothers of James, only Jude is noteworthy. Paul refers to Jude as the "brother of the Lord" (I Corinthians 9:5). According to Matthew's gospel, Jude is one of several brothers of James. Matthew echoes the comments of the people of Nazareth, "Isn't Mary his mother and aren't James, Joseph, Simon, and Judas his brothers? Don't his sisters still live here in our town?" (Matthew 13:55–56). In this listing of brothers, James is mentioned first and Judas or Jude last, possibly because of their ages; also, Jesus had sisters, according to Matthew, though they are not named.

From this sequence, as mentioned, Jude appears to be the youngest brother of the group.

During the ministry of Jesus, Jude is one of the unbelievers (John 7:5). When writing his letter, Jude makes two significant claims: he is a servant of Jesus Christ, and he is a brother of James. Jude recognizes the prominence of his brother James. However, both James and Jude display humility, perhaps not wanting to broadcast their relationship to Jesus. Jude's writing has similar wording as his brother James. Jude relies heavily upon Old Testament sources, and he is extremely interested in the faithful practices of the early Christians.

Jude seems to be more associated with the concerns of Peter regarding the Apocalypse than James. By the time of Jude's letter, the term *a common salvation* is present, and the letter of Jude is placed towards the end of the biblical canon; only the Apocalypse of John follows.

Both James and Jude are concerned with Christians of Jewish background, although both brothers recognize that racial and ethnic barriers have no place in Christianity. Both recognize Jesus their brother as "The Lord Jesus Christ." Both realize the coming parousia of Jesus Christ: "The Lord will soon be here" (James 5:8); "And keep in step with God's love. As you wait for our Lord Jesus Christ to show how kind He is by giving you eternal life" (Jude 21). There is no doubt Jude uses Jewish writings to support his letter, including such writings as the prophecies of Enoch: "The Lord is coming with thousands and thousands of holy angels to judge everyone" (Jude 14–15). Jude also mentions Michael, the Archangel, and his struggle with Satan (Jude 9).

Both James and Jude are extremely concerned with righteous conduct, and both brothers see Jesus Christ a loving and forgiving savior. A careful reading of both letters shows the Jewish heritage of the brothers, very similar to that of Jesus Christ. James seems to be the more practical of the two; Jude delves into ancient sources and appears more esoteric in his viewpoint. Together the brothers capture some of the paradoxical wisdom of their earthly brother and eternal Lord and Savior, Jesus Christ.

# The Last Years of James

As you will recall, James is mentioned in Acts as a leader in the conference where many notable evangelists are gathered. His age at this time is not known, but most scholars place him in the middle age of his life: from 40 to 50 years of age. At this point he is at the peak of his influence in the Jerusalem church. Eusebius, a preeminent early church historian, mentions James as holding the "episcopal seat at Jerusalem." James is married and travels with his wife, according to Paul in I Corinthians 9. James's leadership extends almost to the time of the fall of Jerusalem in 70 AD. Also, according to Eusebius, James is a martyr, as he is stoned to death. This occasion of his death, according to Eusebius, is near the time of the unsuccessful entrapment of Paul who had appealed to Caesar to escape persecution by certain Jewish leaders. This group, after demanding that James renounce Jesus Christ, listens to him declare his faith in Jesus Christ. "But contrary to the sentiments of all, with a firm voice, and much beyond their expectation, he declared himself fully before the multitude, and confirmed that Jesus Christ was the Son of God, Our Savior and Lord."[29]

Craig Evans in his essay "Jesus and James Martyrs of the Temple" constructs a parallel of these two Galilean brothers:

The important point thus far is that two Galilean brothers—Jesus and James—were put to death either indirectly or directly by two high priestly brothers-in-law—Caipaphas and Annas...The line of continuity between Jesus and brother James, the leader of the Jerusalem Church, supports the contention that Jesus and James may very well have advanced the same agenda over against the Temple establishment, and both suffered the same fate at the hands of essentially the same people. In the case of Jesus, of course, due process (in the eyes of Rome) was followed. In the case of James, it was not.[30]

Evans refers to Psalm 118 as a prophetic Psalm and extends the metaphor in the deaths of Jesus and James.

In other references to James in his later years, Painter relies greatly on the historian Eusebius. He states that Eusebius "asserts the leadership of James more or less from the beginning." Painter also emphasizes an important theme of Eusebius, "that the apostles, including Cephas, unanimously elected James as the first bishop of Jerusalem." Eusebius leaves no doubt about the leadership of James in the Jerusalem church. There is no reason why James would have been portrayed in these terms had he not, in fact, been the leader. The tradition is insistent that James is the first, and some attention is focused on his episcopal role and the throne he occupied.[31]

Throughout his leadership role, James associates with Peter, John, and Paul. Were there differences of opinion even after the conference of 50 AD? Tradition records that James is a leader, perhaps the most influential leader in the Jerusalem church until his martyrdom in approximately 62 AD. Painter describes James as the righteous sufferer, which is a part of Jewish belief.[32] James and the Jerusalem church certainly suffer from poverty during the time of his leadership. There is a constant reminder from the letter of James that he has a deep sympathy for the poor and persecuted, which he emphasizes by mentioning the plight of widows and orphans (James 1:27).

As has been mentioned, James does not venture far from Jerusalem and must have dealt on a daily basis with oppression and poverty that plagues the church there. Peter seems to have focused on other locales for his teaching. Markun Bockmuehl concludes that a conference in Antioch becomes pivotal for the early church:

> James' action is consistent with the political desire if possible to secure a modern vivendi for the church in Jerusalem, and with a widely attested religious perspective in which Antioch would be understood in terms of the biblical dimensions of the Lord promised to the Twelve Tribes, who had been the focus of Jesus' mission to Israel. This remains of course no more than a hypothesis, but it is one that may well account for the situation better than many of the more commonly proposed explanations. James' intervention, Peter's accommodation, and Paul's rigid refusal despite being in a minority of one, may each in its own way have contributed to the emergence of a separate group publicly known as Christians— Gentile believers in Christ whose public image could no longer be most obviously identified in association either with pagan cults or as sympathies of the Jewish community. Christianity may well owe its subsequent survival to the fact that it followed neither the Petrine and Jacobean nor indeed the Pauline stance at Antioch, but embraced both the former and the latter together as the apostolic foundation of the Church.[33]

James remains the great facilitator and bulwark of the early church. Paul feels freedom to preach to the Gentiles without interference from Jerusalem. He encourages the Corinthians to collect funds for the less affluent Jewish church in Jerusalem: "Choose some followers to take the money to Jerusalem. I will send them on with the money and with letters which show that you approve of them. If you think I should go along, they can go with me" (I Corinthians 16:3–4).

James and Paul work both together and separately until their parting at the time of James's martyrdom. While Paul is a prisoner in Caesarea, James must have been aware of his imprisonment. However, the circumstances at that time are so dangerous that James could do little, and Paul relies on his Roman citizenship and is safely housed in Caesarea. Earlier, in safer times, Paul visits Jerusalem and is welcomed by James and the church elders. Doubtless James and the other leaders of the church in Jerusalem are pleased because of the generosity of the Gentile churches in helping the church in Jerusalem. F.F. Bruce notices that, by this time of the late 50s AD, James "occupies a leading place in the Jerusalem church. From the absence of all mention of the twelve, it is safe to infer that none of them was in Jerusalem at this time." Bruce mentions the tradition of both Clement and Eusebius that the Lord commands the apostles to stay twelve years in Jerusalem and then go out into the entire world. [34]

Paul's meeting with James is at this time is perhaps their last encounter (Acts 21). Again, Bruce states that the Jerusalem leaders have cause to "praise God not only for the conversion of the Gentiles, but also for the practical evidence of their concession in the contribution sent to the Jerusalem Christians."[35] The riot that occurs in Jerusalem during this visit is targeting Paul and conducted by Asian Jews. Paul gives a superb apologia in Acts 22 and is rescued from an angry mob by Roman soldiers. There can be no doubt that James and the other Jerusalem leaders are aware of this riot, but they are unable to help.

Before this, James provides advice and urges Paul to observe Jewish customs and pay money for a communal Nazarite vow. Luke, who witnesses the proceedings, writes, "The next day Paul took the four men with him and got himself ready at the same time they did. Then he went into the temple and told when the final ceremony would take place and when an offering would be made for each of them" (Acts 21:26).

Through this advice, James is encouraging Paul to appease an angry group who were in Jerusalem for the religious festival. These Jews are from Ephesus and recognize an Ephesian who is a Gentile and who is with Paul. Paul in the superb address to this angry group states his own Jewish credentials, but also mentions his mission to the Gentile world (Acts 22). Again, it would have been impossible for James to stop this mob, and only military force saves Paul from harm.

James, who is nearing the end of his church influence, observes that Jewish customs are diminishing in the church. As Bruce Chilton writes, James is practical or pragmatic. Within the decade of the end of his service, he sees profound changes. He does not see the destruction of the Temple or the cessation of the Nazarite vow, but the influence of Paul and the conversion of the Gentile world are very near. Peter is now to live in the shadow of James who once advised him and had steered a steady course for the merging of Christians from various ethnic backgrounds. Chilton adds that "the rules set by James naturally to separate believing Gentiles from their ambient environment" are present.[36]

Until his final hours, James preaches purity and holiness with devotion to the teachings of God—no matter if one is Jew or Gentile. His last days end in his death because of his faith in Jesus Christ. The Jerusalem church loses its greatest leader.

# Final Thoughts

Many people were quite unaware of the significance of James until certain information began appearing in issues of *Biblical Archaeological Review* in the early 2000s. *BAR*, as it is often called, ran a series of articles written mostly by Hershel Shanks, the editor of the magazine. The articles allege that the ossuary or coffin of James was located in Jerusalem by Oded Golan, an antiquities dealer in Jerusalem. An ossuary is a stone casket that preserved the skeletal remains of Jews. The ossuary of James was discovered in 2002 and immediately caused a stir in the archaeological world as well as with Christian scholars.

After much testimony from both believers and skeptics, Shanks wrote an article entitled "Brother of Jesus Inscription is Authentic." The controversy continued for years, and Shanks wrote another article in 2012 on the authenticity of the ossuary: "Is the inscription authentic? The court held only that the prosecution failed to prove beyond a reasonable doubt that the inscription was a forgery. But it surely did not find that the inscription was authentic. I have no doubt, however, that it is."[37] Shanks is referring to the claim that Golan had forged the inscription "James, Son of Joseph, Brother of Jesus" on the ossuary. The ossuary's age, approximately 2000 years, was not seriously contested by the courts.

To support the authenticity, Shanks's article quotes such authorities as Andre

Lemaire and Ada Yardeni who agree that the inscription is authentic; the author also includes doubters such as Eric Meyers, former president of The American School of Oriental Research. Shanks relentlessly persists that the ossuary in question contains the remains of James, the brother of Jesus. Shanks even consults statisticians such as Professor Camil Fuchs of Tel Aviv University. Fuchs concludes that there is a very small chance that all three names, Joseph, James, and Jesus, would be inscribed on the same ossuary.[38]

Regardless of the conclusion one reaches, the discovery of the ossuary brought new attention to James among the masses of people who had heard very little about him. When one reads the New Testament, James is held in prominence. The writers of the New Testament begin by placing James as the first of several brothers and sisters in the family of Jesus (Matthew 13:54–56). Some commentators have expressed the idea that James was the son of Joseph by an earlier marriage. However, as mentioned earlier, the overwhelming belief among the Protestant academic world is that James was the son of Joseph and Mary, a belief supported by the marriage consummation mentioned in Matthew 1:24–25. As J. W. Roberts observes, "Tertullian, one of the early patristic writers, argued from the evidence of Joseph and Mary's children that 'the sanctity of marriage is hallowed by the mother of Jesus living in wedlock and bearing children after the birth of Jesus.'"[39]

In the adult years of James, the perplexing question of his alleged disbelief in the Messiah's role of Jesus continues to intrigue: "Even Jesus' own brothers had not yet become his followers" (John 7:5). Painter helps clarify this apparent mystery:

> From the Johannine perspective, belief prior to the resurrection/ glorification of Jesus is thought to be suspect, so that right at the end of his farewell discourses Jesus challenges the affirmation of belief by the disciples, "Do you now believe?" (John 16:31). If Jesus puts the belief of the disciples in question at this point, we would hesitate before concluding that the narrator's comment in 7:5 indicates that the brothers were total unbelievers. By Johannine standards of "authentic" or ideal belief neither the disciples nor the brothers qualified until after the resurrection of Jesus and the coming of the Paraclete.[40]

James is as the other followers of Jesus. He is unsure of the role of Jesus and unsure of His mission. James possesses no unusual predilection concerning Jesus, simply because He is his brother. However, once the resurrection is known to James as well as to others, the puzzle fits together. His closeness to Jesus during their youth becomes a supreme advantage in his relationship to the nascent church.

James's greatest contribution, at least in the beginning years of the Gospel, is his leadership at the Jerusalem conference. At this time one can picture James as a mature Christian, acknowledged by all the early church leaders as a person of great wisdom and discernment. To say that he keeps the Christian communities together in purpose and thought would be no exaggeration. Paul later has to deal with the "parties" of Peter and Apollos at Corinth. Paul may remember the exaltation of Christ in all things shown by James in Jerusalem. Obviously the conciliatory message of James rings true and guides these various leaders of the early church:

> My friends listen to me! Simon Peter has told how God first
> came to the Gentiles and made some of them His own people.
> This agrees with what the prophets wrote, "I, the Lord, will
> return and rebuild David's fallen house, I will build it from its
> ruins and set it up again. Then other nations will turn to me
> and be my chosen ones. I, the Lord, say this, I promised it
> long ago." (Acts 15:13–18)

As F.F. Bruce comments about the "ten skenen" of David, "the church is the legitimate continuation of the old Church of Israel. We need not be surprised to find James, a Galilean, speaking Gk. and quoting from the LXX, especially in the presence of the 'certain others' from Antioch whose language would be Gk. It has been pointed out in this connection that the OT quotations in the Epistle of James are nearly all from the LXX."[41] Therefore, James, through a quotation from the Old Testament prophet Amos, reconciles ethnic differences and, as Chilton states, practices a theological pragmatism that saves primitive Christianity. Chilton quotes from Amos 9:11–12, "After this I will come back and restore the tent of David which has fallen and rebuild its ruins and set it up anew, that the rest of men may seek the Lord, and all the Gentiles upon whom my name is called." Chilton adds, "In the argument of James as represented here, what the belief of Gentiles achieves is, not the redefinition of Israel (as in Paul's thought), but the restoration of the house of David. The argument is possible because Davidic genealogy of Jesus—and, therefore, of his brother James—is assumed."[42] James is portrayed by the church leaders as the wise arbiter of the Christian faith. Differences occur as they will always occur in the thoughts of God's elect, but the wisdom of James finally prevails.

James through his life and letter has had a strong impact on Christianity. It can be argued that Christian vitality and social relevance in the modern world owes a great deal to James and his teachings. J.W. Roberts writes, "James insists that the word must be a vital factor. It must be active in both positive and negative ways in our lives, in good deeds, and in morality."[43] As mentioned, James, perhaps more than any other New Testament writer, emphasizes the need for prayer:

> If you are having trouble you should pray. And if you are feeling good, you should sing praises…If you are sick, ask the church leaders to come and pray for you, and then to put olive oil on you in the name of the Lord. If you have faith when you pray for sick people, they will get well. The Lord will heal them, and if they have sinned, he will forgive them. (James 5:13–15)

James continues with confession as part of prayer:

> If you have sinned, you should tell each other what you have done. They can pray for one another and be healed. The prayer of an innocent person is powerful, and it can help a lot. Elijah was just as human as we are, and for three and a half years his prayers kept the rain from falling. But when he did pray for rain, it fell from the skies and made the crops grow. (James 5:16–18)

J.W. Roberts extends the prayer of James to the repentance of the sinner: "James may be thinking of the many Jews who, now that the Judaism of their fathers had begun to harden against Christianity, were finding the way difficult. He may remember that he himself had once not believed in the claims of his brother Jesus."[44]

James's New Testament life began as a doubter of Jesus; his life in the scriptures and in historical tradition ends with a strong confidence that demonstrates works of faith and a great social conscience towards the needy of body and soul. He becomes the most visible of the leaders of the Jerusalem church, a mentor and adviser to the great evangelists of his time as he fights the egregious impurities of the pagan world. Above all, this brother of Jesus exercises great humility towards God and his fellow Christians accompanied with a great zeal towards the salvation of the lost souls of his generation.

"My friends, if any followers have wandered away from the truth, you should try to lead them back. If you turn sinners from the wrong way, you will save them from death" (James 5:19-20a).

# Addendum

## *The Martyrdom of James, the brother of Jesus*

Martyrdom of prominent believers affects the early church in many ways. R. B. Rackham notes that "the death of Stephen was the crucial event which started the expansion of the church. The blood of the martyr was the seed of the church." As the Christians scatter during this first persecution, "They evangelized or preached the word. Thus as the chief strength of Judaism, both political and intellectual, lay in its Dispersion or Scattering abroad, so the new Dispersion of the Christians formed the progressive and missionary element in the church." Stephen sees "Jesus standing as Prophet and Mediator between God and man."[45]

The martyrdom of Stephen is the most dramatic of these early sacrificial deaths because it is the first recorded in the gospel narratives, and certainly because of Stephen's eloquent address. Other early martyrdoms follow. The missionary activity of Peter and James and John continues to be an influence in the Jerusalem area until this effort is violently interrupted by the execution of James, the son of Zebedee, described briefly by Luke in the Book of Acts.

Bruce, in his book *The Spreading Flame*, comments on this occurrence:

> It is remarkable, indeed, how little we know about the later career
> of most of the twelve apostles. James, the son of Zebedee, we
> know, was executed in Jerusalem under Herod Agrippa I in 44, we
> can trace the movements of his brother John from time to time,
> and we can reconstruct the outline of Peter's later life with consid-
> erable probability. But what do we know of Andrew and Thomas
> and Matthew, Philip and Bartholomew, James the son of Alpheus
> and Judas the son of James, Simon the Zealot, and Matthias, the
> successor of Judas Iscariot? Legend is lavish in its willingness to
> tell us what became of them, but we have amazingly little histori-
> cal knowledge. They do not appear to have remained in Jerusalem
> after the middle of the first century.[46]

Regarding Stephen's execution, Bruce considers this martyr and his message a
threat to the powerful Jewish Sanhedrin:

> Stephen's assertion that the temple and the priesthood and ev-
> erything associated with them were doomed to extinction formed
> the basis of a charge of blasphemy brought against him before
> the Sanhedrin. When called upon to make his defense he simply
> reiterated the arguments which he had used in the synagogue, and
> at last he was hustled out of the council chamber and stoned to
> death. Paul thoroughly approved of this proceeding, and showed
> his approval by guarding the clothes of the witnesses in the case,
> who (in accordance with Jewish practices) acted as chief execu-
> tioners.

Bruce concludes that this martyrdom fires the repressive actions taken against
the "Nazarenes" and invigorates the zealous career of Paul against this new
doctrine and its adherents. This persecuted group, who is later called Christians, leaves Jerusalem "for other parts of Judea and some even crossed the
boundaries of Palestine into Syria and Phoenicia and other neighboring
states and provinces."[47]

Bruce considers the execution of Stephen similar to James the brother of Jesus. James is executed without the Roman Procurators approval. But procurators had established a modus vivendi for dealing with the Jewish religious leaders. As procurators lived in Caesarea "once strong feelings were stirred up in Jerusalem, they were not easily curbed."[48]

Of course at times the Jewish ruler plays an important part in the execution of Christians. Rackham offers as an example the execution of a different James, the son of Zebedee. To study this martyrdom, one must be familiar with the infamous Herod Agrippa I.[49] Rackham describes this Herod as the "grandson of Herod the Great" and as one who "had been brought up at Rome in intimate relations with the imperial family. He had become a great friend of the young Caligula; and while this friendship brought him in danger of his life under Tiberius, it made his fortune at the ascension of Caligula."[50] After the death of Caligula, Agrippa is "instrumental in getting the senate to accept Claudius as his successor, and the grateful emperor added to Agrippa's kingdom Judea and Samaria. Agrippa had hitherto remained at Rome, where he had been notorious chiefly for his prodigality and extravagance. Now he returned to his kingdom of Judea, and there, in order to gain the favour of the Jews, he displayed the greatest assiduity in the observance of the law and the exhibition of external righteousness."[51] Agrippa finds an easy target to curry this favor by persecuting the "Nazarenes," and the persecution is obviously aimed at church leaders such as James and John (sons of Zebedee), Peter, and James, the brother of Jesus.

Regarding James of Zebedee, Rackham observes:

> This is the only place, outside of the last of the twelve, where he
> is mentioned in the Acts. We are struck with the brief notice
> given to an event which in our eyes would be so important—the
> martyrdom of an apostle. It is of a piece with the silence about the
> details of Stephen's persecution, and about the deaths of the other
> apostles; and reflects the true instincts of the early church. In days
> of ardent faith and also of expectation of the Lord's speedy return,
> death sank into its true place as simply a change of condition;
> at the worst it was but a falling asleep. Accordingly instead of
> dealing with morbid interest on the painful details of the martyr's

sufferings, the church pressed forward to reap with joy the harvest of their blood.[52]

The other significant martyrdom in the gospels is the execution of John the Baptist. Since John's death is not directly connected with his following Jesus Christ, it can be said that he is technically executed prior to the Christian martyrs. The Gospel of Matthew records perhaps the most complete account of the Baptist's execution. Herod Antipas, the Herodian ruler that Jesus calls a fox in Luke 13:32, imprisons John because John reveals to him that it is morally wrong to marry Herodias, the wife of his brother Philip (Mark 6:17). Herod Antipas deeply resents this accusation and wants to kill John, but he is afraid of the followers of John who believe John is an esteemed prophet.

> When Herod's birthday came, the daughter of Herodias danced for the guests. She pleased Herod so much that he swore to give her whatever she wanted. But the girl's mother told her to say, "Here on a platter I want the head of John the Baptist!" The king was sorry for what he had said. But he did not want to break the promise he had made in front of his guests. So he ordered a guard to go to the prison and cut off John's head. It was taken to the girl, and she gave it to her mother. John's followers took his body and buried it. Then they told Jesus what had happened. (Matthew 14:8–12)

Mark is very specific about Herodias holding a deep grudge against John. She wants to kill John, but is prevented because Herod is afraid of John and protects him (Mark 6:19–20). Herod knows that John is a holy man. Even though Herod is not pleased with what John is saying about him, he listens. Finally Herodias gets her chance when Herod gives himself the birthday celebration that Matthew mentions. Mark points out that Herod's officials, army officers, and the leaders of Galilee are there at the feast before he repeats Matthew's description of the dance and the request (6:21–29).

In the view of these gospel writers, John the Baptist becomes a martyr, the first in the time of Christ. Careful analysis shows that, in the tradition of the

Old Testament prophets, he is executed for condemning open sin. One can now move to an examination of the execution of James, the brother of Jesus, which is not recorded in the New Testament.

Eusebius in his *Ecclesiastical History* describes James as the Just, one who is consecrated before his birth. James is described as one who lives as a Nazarite: one who uses no razor, abstains from strong drink, and never uses public baths. He also engages in prayer so often that his knees become hardened. Eusebius relies heavily on Hegesippus, an early patristic writer, for these observations.

According to Eusebius, James is encouraged by Jewish leaders to denounce Jesus' claim to be the Christ. This occurs during the time of the Passover observance in the early 60s AD. The scribes and Pharisees place James on the "wing of the temple" where James is to denounce Jesus as the Christ. However, James will not comply. James comments, "Why do ye ask me respecting Jesus the Son of Man? He is now sitting in the heavens, on the right hand of great Power, and is about to come on the clouds of heaven." In Eusebius's account, this seals the fate of James, who is then stoned by the Scribes and Pharisees who are there. Eusebius adds that James is also clubbed with a heavy object to ensure his death. "So admirable a man indeed was James, and so celebrated among all for his justice, that even the wiser part of the Jews were of opinion that this was the cause of the immediate siege of Jerusalem, which happened to them for no other reason than the crime against him."[53]

The execution of Paul occurs a few years later than James according to secular history. Bruce, in his lengthy biography of Paul called *Paul: Apostle of the Heart Set Free*, concludes that Paul also suffers execution in the 60s AD: "That Paul's life was brought to an end in Rome by the executioner's sword may be confidently accepted, but tradition associates his execution with the persecution of Christians in Rome which followed the great fire of A.D. 64— at least two years after the latest probable date for the hearing of his case."[54] This hearing is part of Paul's appeal to Caesar. Bruce also refers to Clement, a patristic writer who lived nearly 40 years later after Paul's death and who refers to the great persecution of Christians under Nero.[55] William Ramsay, another Pauline scholar, accepts the tradition that Paul is executed by the Romans on the road to Ostia, Rome's great seaport, in the 60s AD.[56]

Thus, according to very reliable secular historical sources, the lives of two great Christian leaders, James and Paul, end in the same decade of the first century. As the great biblical scholar John R.W. Stott looks back at the days of the Jerusalem Compromise, he concludes, "Paul and James can be reconciled in their New Testament letters too. They taught the same way of salvation." He adds that the Jerusalem conference is a legacy for both leaders and "secured a double victory—a victory of truth in conferring the gospel of grace, and a victory of love in preserving the fellowship of sensitive concessions to conscientious Jewish scruples."[57] Succeeding years have proven this assessment of James to be true as he was as devoted to his brother Jesus in death as he was in life.

"My friends, be glad, even if you have a lot of trouble. You know that you learn to endure by having your faith tested…God will bless you, if you don't give up when your faith is being tested. He will reward you with a glorious life" (James 1:2–3, 12a).

# Notes

1. Louis Matthew Sweet, *International Standard Bible Encyclopedia*, "Mary," Wm. B. Eerdmans Publishing Company, Grand Rapids, Michigan, 1960

2. Alfred Plummer. *The Exegetical Commentary on the Gospel According to S. Matthew,* Wm.B. Eerdmans Publishing Company, Grand Rapids, Michigan, 1956

3. Ibid

4. B.F. Westcott, *The Gospel According to St. John*, Wm. B. Eerdmans Publishing Company, Grand Rapids, Michigan, 1958

5. Frederick Louis Godet, *Commentary on the Gospel of John*, Zondervan Publishing House, Grand Rapids, Michigan, 1881

6. John Painter, *Just James, The Brother of Jesus in History and Tradition*, University of South Carolina Press, Columbia, South Carolina, 1997

7. Ibid

8. Leon Morris, *The Gospel of John*, Eerdmans Publishing House, Grand Rapids, Michigan, 1979

9. Henry Wansborough, *Luke Doubleday Bible Commentary*, Doubleday, New York, 1998

10. F.F. Bruce, *The Acts of the Apostles*, The Tyndale Press, London, 1956

11. R.B. Rackham, *The Acts of the Apostles*, Metheun and Co.Ltd., London, 1957

12. F.F. Bruce, *The Acts of the Apostles*, The Tyndale Press, London, 1956

13. Ibid

14. Scott McKnight, *The Brother of Jesus: James the Just and His Mission*, John Knox Press, Louisville, 2001

15. John Painter, *Just James, The Brother of Jesus in History and Tradition*, University of South Carolina Press, Columbia, South Carolina, 1997

16. William Farmer, *The Brother of Jesus: James the Just and His Mission*, John Knox Press, Louisville, 2001

17. F.F. Bruce, *The Spreading Flame*, The Paternoster Press, London, 1961

18. Ibid

19. Ibid

20. Ibid

21. J.W. Roberts, *The Letter of James*, The Sweet Publishing Company, Austin, Texas, 1977

22. Ibid

23. W.E. Oesterley, *The General Epistle of James, The Expositors Greek Testament*, Wm. B. Eerdmans Publishing Company, Grand Rapids, Michigan, 1956

24. Ibid

25. J.W. Roberts, *The Letter of James*, The Sweet Publishing Company, Austin, Texas, 1977

26. John Painter, *Just James, The Brother of Jesus in History and Tradition*, University of South Carolina Press, Columbia, South Carolina, 1997

27. J.W. Roberts, *The Letter of James*, The Sweet Publishing Company, Austin, Texas, 1977

28. John Painter, *Just James, The Brother of Jesus in History and Tradition*, University of South Carolina Press, Columbia, South Carolina, 1997

29. Eusebius, *Ecclesiastical History*, Hendrickson Publishing, Peabody, Massachusetts, 1998

30. Craig Evans, *The Brother of Jesus: James the Just and His Mission*, John Knox Press, Louisville, 2001

31. Eusebius, *Ecclesiastical History*, Hendrickson Publishing, Peabody, Massachusetts, 1998

32. John Painter, *Just James, The Brother of Jesus in History and Tradition*, University of South Carolina Press, Columbia, South Carolina, 1997

33. Markun Bockmuehl, *The Brother of Jesus: James the Just and His Mission*, John Knox Press, Louisville, 2001

34. F.F. Bruce, *The Spreading Flame*, The Paternoster Press, London, 1961

35. Ibid

36. Bruce Chilton, *The Brother of Jesus: James the Just and His Mission*, John Knox Press, Louisville, 2001

37. Hershel Shanks, *Biblical Archaeological Review*, Washington, D.C., 2012

38. Ibid

39. J.W. Roberts, *The Letter of James*, The Sweet Publishing Company, Austin, Texas, 1977

40. John Painter, *Just James, The Brother of Jesus in History and Tradition*, University of South Carolina Press, Columbia, South Carolina, 1997

41. F.F. Bruce, *The Spreading Flame*, The Paternoster Press, London, 1961

42. Bruce Chilton, *The Brother of Jesus: James the Just and His Mission*, John Knox Press, Louisville, 2001

43. J.W. Roberts, *The Letter of James*, The Sweet Publishing Company, Austin, Texas, 1977

44. Ibid

45. R.B.Rackham, *The Acts of the Apostles*, Metheun and Co. Ltd., London, 1957

46. F.F. Bruce, *The Spreading Flame*, The Paternoster Press, London, 1961

47. Ibid

48. Ibid

49. Ibid

50. R.B. Rackham, *The Acts of the Apostles*, Metheun and Co. Ltd., London, 1957

51. Ibid

52. Ibid

53. Eusebius, *Ecclesiastical History*, Hendrickson Publishing, Peabody, Massachusetts, 1998

54. F.F. Bruce, *The Apostle of the Heart Set Free*, Wm. B. Eerdmans Publishing Company, Grand Rapids, Michigan, 1984

55. Ibid

56. William Ramsay, *St. Paul, The Traveler and Roman Citizen*, Kregel Publications, Grand Rapids, Michigan, 2001

57. J.R.W. Stott, *The Message of Acts*, Inter-Varsity Press, Downers Grove, Illinois, 1990

# About the Author

**James Byers** is a graduate of David Lipscomb College, magna cum laude, and teaches an Asian Bible class at Harpeth Hills Church of Christ where he serves as a deacon. He has been a minister in congregations in Tennessee, Georgia, Florida, and Hawaii. He had a career with the State of Tennessee as a teacher in Williamson County and with the Department of Human Services. He is married to the former Marie Potter, and they have one son, Tracy Byers, who is married to the former Evie Wade. James and Marie are also proud grandparents of three grandchildren. This is his fourth book.

# Other Books by the Author

# Angels of Great Joy
## God's Messengers of the Nativity

### James Byers

# Angels of Great Joy:
# God's Messengers of the Nativity
## ISBN 978-0-9860244-1-2

The New Testament begins with an explosion of heavenly messengers–angels of joy with glorious announcements. Angels told of the birth and parts of the infancy narrative. These proclamations came to the humble of spirit: a country priest, lowly shepherds of Bethlehem, a Galilean carpenter, and a maiden from Nazareth. Filled with hope, comfort, and praise to God, the promises shared a beautiful truth: the fulfillment of Isaiah 9:6. "Unto us a child is born...His name will be Wonderful."

# THE APOSTLE JOHN

## a blessed life

**James Byers**

# The Apostle John: A Blessed Life
# by James Byers
ISBN-13: 978-0-9800285-2-2

*The Apostle John: A Blessed Life* takes a historical and philosophical look into the life and work of this son of Zebedee. Once a "son of thunder," John's spiritual journey led him to become the man called to write a special, personal account of the life of Jesus. This book guides the reader through the world in which John lived and the gospel, letters, and revelation tale written with divine direction and his unique perspective.

From his days fishing with his father and brother on the Sea of Galilee, to his travels with Jesus, and finally to his last days writing and sharing Christ's word in Ephesus, this apostle truly lived a blessed life.

# Hope of Heaven

## Expectations and Descriptions

James Byers

# Hope of Heaven

ISBN 978-0-9822618-7-3

"I have prepared a place for you, in My Father's house where there are many dwelling places" (John 14:2). With these words Jesus encouraged His disciples, and future Christians, of a glorious heaven. His first coming made this hope of heaven possible; His final coming will make it complete.

This book explores some of the expectations and descriptions of heaven throughout the Bible. Christ will come. His eternal kingdom shall be established. This is the great hope and fear of all generations.

To order copies, contact the author or visit www.hilliardinstitute.com.

www.ingramcontent.com/pod-product-compliance
Lightning Source LLC
Chambersburg PA
CBHW020951030426
42339CB00004B/47